NATIONAL GEOGRAPHIC OUR WORLD

WORKBOOK
STARTER

SERIES EDITORS
JoAnn (Jodi) Crandall
Joan Kang Shin

AUTHOR
Diane Pinkley

Unit 0		2
Unit 1	My School	5
Unit 2	My Toys	9
Unit 3	My Family	13
Unit 4	My Body	17
Units 1–4 Review		21
Unit 5	Stories	23
Unit 6	I Like Food	27
Unit 7	Clothes	31
Unit 8	Animals	35
Units 5–8 Review		39
Writing		41
Cutouts		57

NATIONAL GEOGRAPHIC LEARNING | **CENGAGE Learning**

Australia • Brazil • Japan • Korea • Mexico • Singapore • Spain • United Kingdom • United States

Unit 0

1 **Listen.** Look and circle. TR: 2

1.

2.

3.

2 **Listen and circle.** TR: 3

1.    yes   no

2.    yes   no

3.    yes   no

3 **Listen.** Color and say. TR: 4

1.

2.

4 **Listen.** Color and say. TR: 5

5 **Look.** Count and write.

6 **Listen.** Draw and color. TR: 6

7 **Listen and say.** TR: 7

8 **Listen and look.** Which word is different? Circle. TR: 8

1.

2.

9 **Listen and chant.** Point. TR: 9

Hello, hello.
Hi there, hi.

Time to go.
Bye, goodbye!

Unit 1
My School

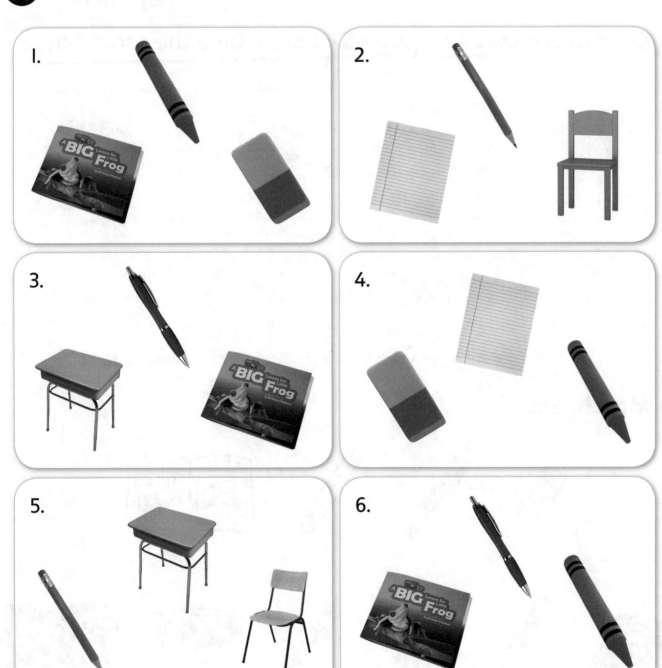

1.

2.

3.

4.

5.

6.

2 **Listen and say.** TR: 11

3 **Cut out the cards on page 57.** Listen. Glue the cards. Say. TR: 12

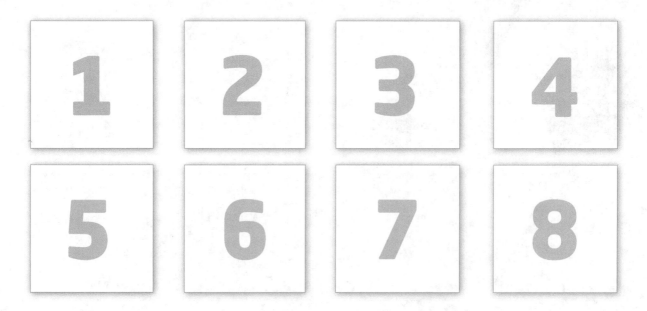

4 **Match.** Say.

5 **Listen.** Color and say. TR: 13

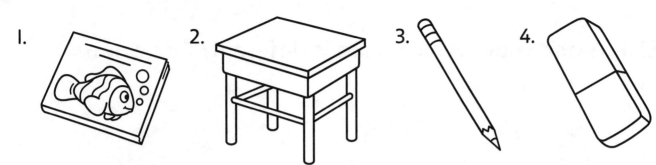

1.   2.   3.   4.

6 **Listen.** Color. Count and say. TR: 14

7 **Listen.** Count and write. TR: 15

8 **Listen and say.** TR: 16

9 **Listen and look.** Which word is different? Circle. TR: 17

1.

2.

3.

10 **Listen and chant.** Say a new verse. TR: 18

I have some

I have a

I have a

Let's draw again!

I have an

I have a

I have some

Let's draw again!

Unit 2
My Toys

1 **Listen.** Look and circle. TR: 19

1.

2.

3.

4.

5.

6.

2 **Listen and say.** TR: 20

3 **Cut out the cards on page 57.** Listen. What is it? Glue the cards. Say. TR: 21

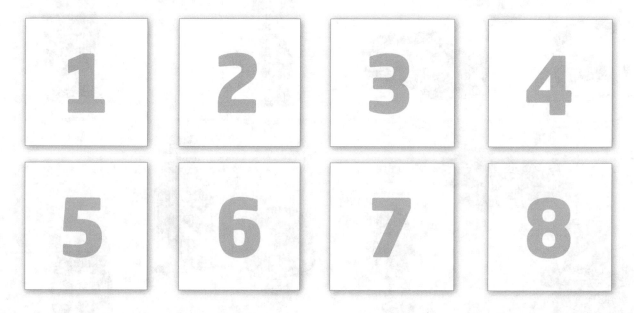

4 **Draw your favorite toy.** Color. What is it? Say.

5 **Listen.** Color and say. TR: 22

1.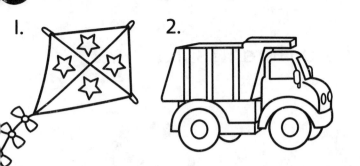
2.
3.
4.

6 **Listen.** Color. Count and say. TR: 23

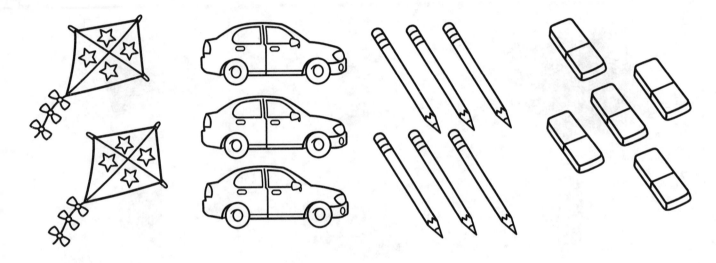

7 **Listen.** Count and write. TR: 24

8 **Listen and say.** TR: 25

9 **Listen and look.** Which word is different? Circle. TR: 26

1.

2.

3.

10 **Listen and chant.** Say a new verse. TR: 27

and
and more toys.
and
for girls and boys!

and
and more toys.
and
for girls and boys!

Unit 3
My Family

1 **Listen and look.** Draw a line. TR: 28

1
2
3
4
5
6
7
8
9
10

2 **Listen and say.** TR: 29

Who's this?

It's my sister.

3 **Listen and circle.** TR: 30

1.   2.   3.

4 **Listen and say.** TR: 31

Where's Mother?

In the living room

5 **Cut out the cards on page 59.** Listen. Where's the family? Glue the cards. Say. TR: 32

6 **Listen.** Color and say. TR: 33

1.
2.
3.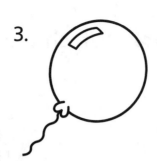
4.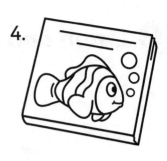

7 **Listen.** Color. Count and say. TR: 34

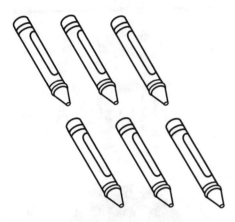 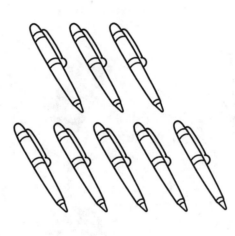 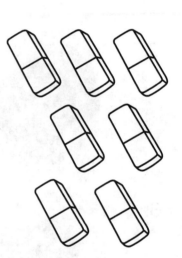

8 **Listen.** Count and write. TR: 35

9 **Listen and say.** TR: 36

10 **Listen and look.** Which word is different? Circle. TR: 37

1.

2.

3.

11 **Listen and chant.** Say a new verse. TR: 38

I love my

Oh yes, I do.

My   and my

love him, too.

I love my

Oh yes, I do.

My   and my

love her, too.

Unit 4
My Body

1 **Listen and look.** Draw a line. TR: 39

1

2

3

4

5

6

7

8

9

17

2 **Listen and say.** TR: 40

I have 4 feet.

He has 4 feet.

3 **Listen and circle.** Say. TR: 41

1.

2.

3.

4.

4 **Cut out the cards on page 59.** Listen and look.
Glue the cards. Say. TR: 42

| 1 | 2 | 3 | 4 |

5 **Listen.** Color and say. TR: 43

1.  2.  3.  4.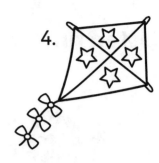

6 **Listen.** Color. Count and say. TR: 44

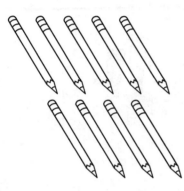 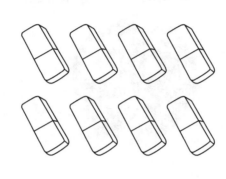 

7 **Listen.** Count and write. TR: 45

19

8 **Listen and say.** TR: 46

9 **Listen and look.** Which word is different? Circle. TR: 47

1.

2.

3.

10 **Listen and chant.** Say a new verse. TR: 48

One ⌣ for me.

Two 🙋 for you.

Two 👀 for me.

Two 🧦 for you.

No 👴 for me.

Brown 💇 for you.

A 👃 for me,

and 🥸 , too.

mustache

Units 1-4

Review

1 **Listen.** Look and circle. TR: 49

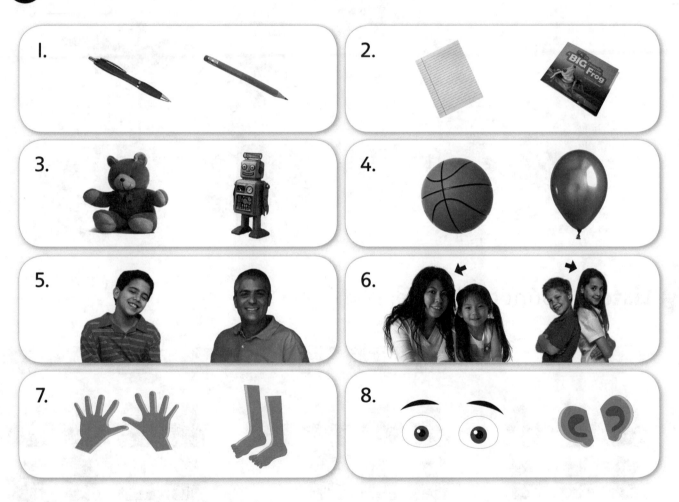

1.

2.

3.

4.

5.

6.

7.

8.

2 **Listen and color.** TR: 50

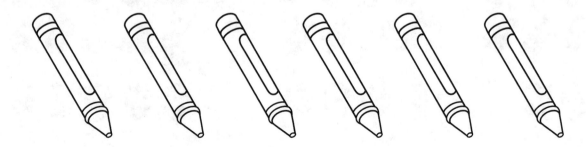

3 **Listen.** Look and circle. **TR: 51**

4 **Listen.** Count and circle. **TR: 52**

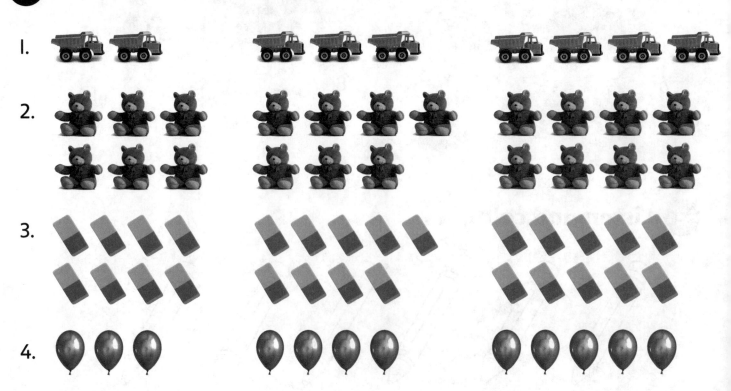

Unit 5
Stories

1 **Listen.** Look and circle. TR: 53

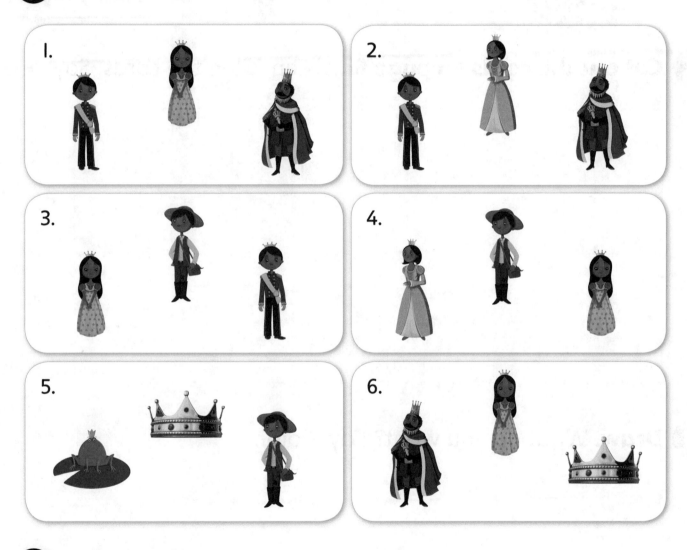

2 **Listen.** Draw. TR: 54

1.

2.

3 **Listen and say.** TR: 55

4 **Cut out the cards on page 61.** Listen. Glue the cards. Say. TR: 56

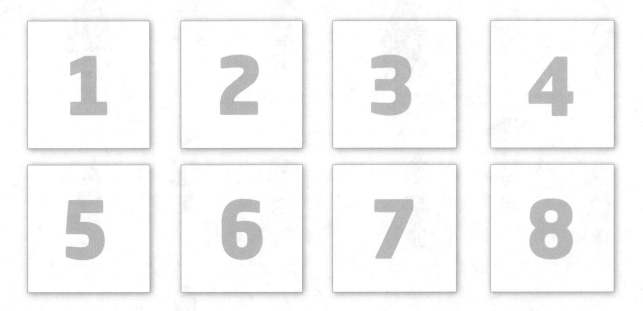

5 **Draw.** What do you want? Say. Color.

6 **Listen.** Color and say. TR: 57

1.
2.
3.
4.

7 **Listen.** Color. Count and say. TR: 58

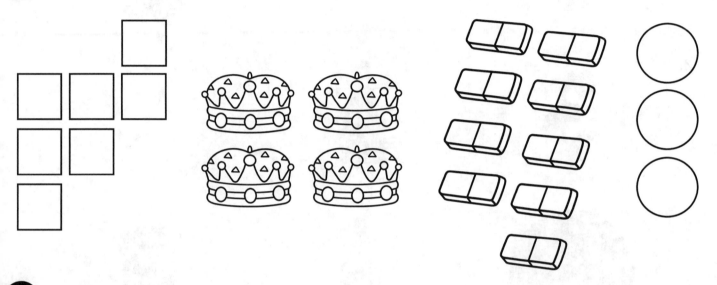

8 **Listen.** Count and write. TR: 59

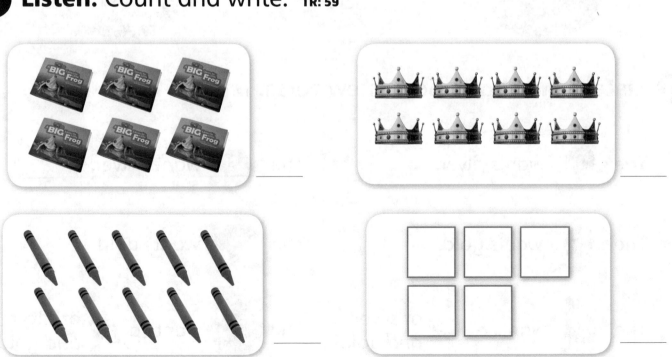

9 **Listen and say.** TR: 60

10 **Listen and look.** Which word is different? Circle. TR: 61

1.

2.

3.

11 **Listen and chant.** Say a new verse. TR: 62

The wants silver.

The wants gold.

The wants a of silver *and* gold!

The wants silver.

The wants gold.

The wants a ring of silver *and* gold!

Unit 6
I Like Food

1 **Listen.** Look and circle. TR: 63

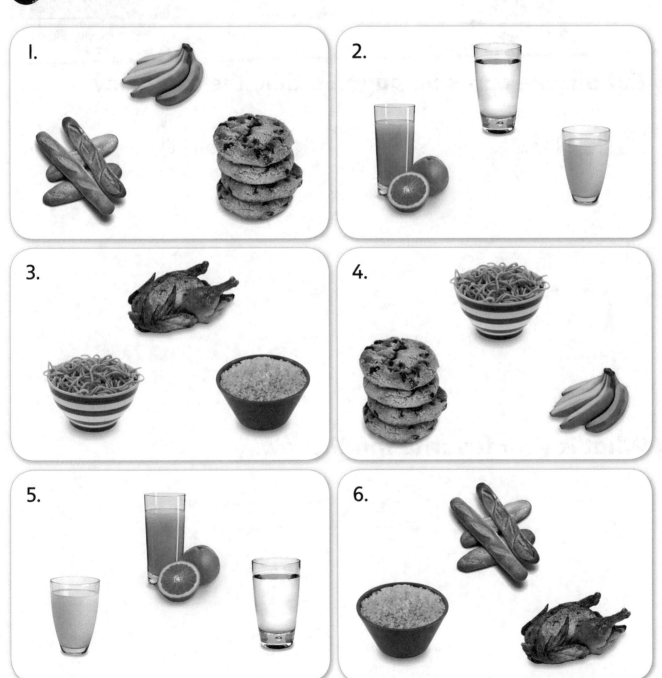

1.

2.

3.

4.

5.

6.

2 Listen and say. TR: 64

I like orange juice.

I don't like orange juice. I like milk.

3 Cut out the cards on page 61. Glue the cards. Say.

🙂 I like...

☹ I don't like...

4 What is your favorite food? Draw.

5 **Listen and color.** Listen, count, and say. TR: 65

1.

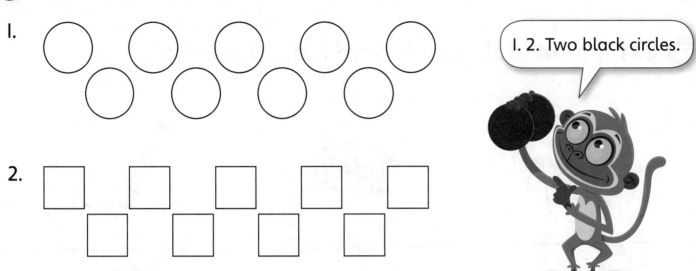

I. 2. Two black circles.

2.

6 **Count and say.** How many circles? How many squares?

circles _____

squares _____

7 **Listen.** Count and say. TR: 66

8 **Listen and say.** TR: 67

9 **Listen and look.** Which word is different? Circle. TR: 68

1.

2.

3.

10 **Listen and chant.** Say a new verse. TR: 69

I like

I like

I like

They're so nice!

I like

I like

I like

They're so nice!

Unit 7
Clothes

1 **Listen and look.** Draw a line. TR: 70

2 **Listen and look.** Draw a line. Color. TR: 71

3 **Listen and say.** TR: 72

It's hot. I'm wearing shorts.

It's cold. He's wearing a hat.

4 **Cut out the cards on page 63.** Listen. Glue the cards. Say. TR: 73

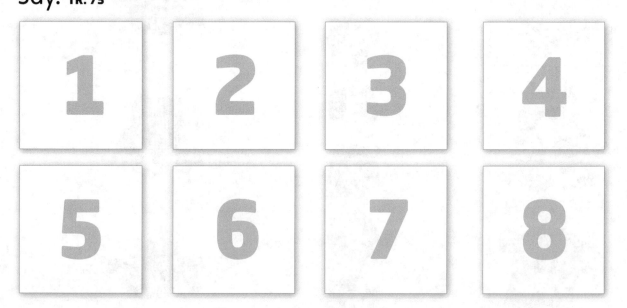

| 1 | 2 | 3 | 4 |
| 5 | 6 | 7 | 8 |

5 **Connect the dots.** What is it? Say. Color.

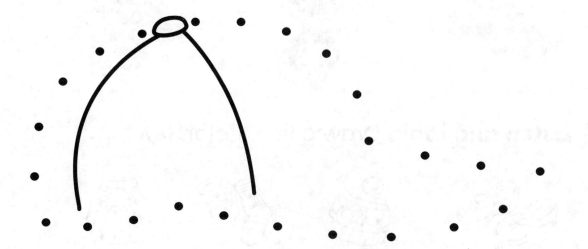

6 **Listen.** Color and say. **TR: 74**

1. 2. 3. 4.

7 **Listen.** Color. Count and say. **TR: 75**

8 **Listen.** Count and write. **TR: 76**

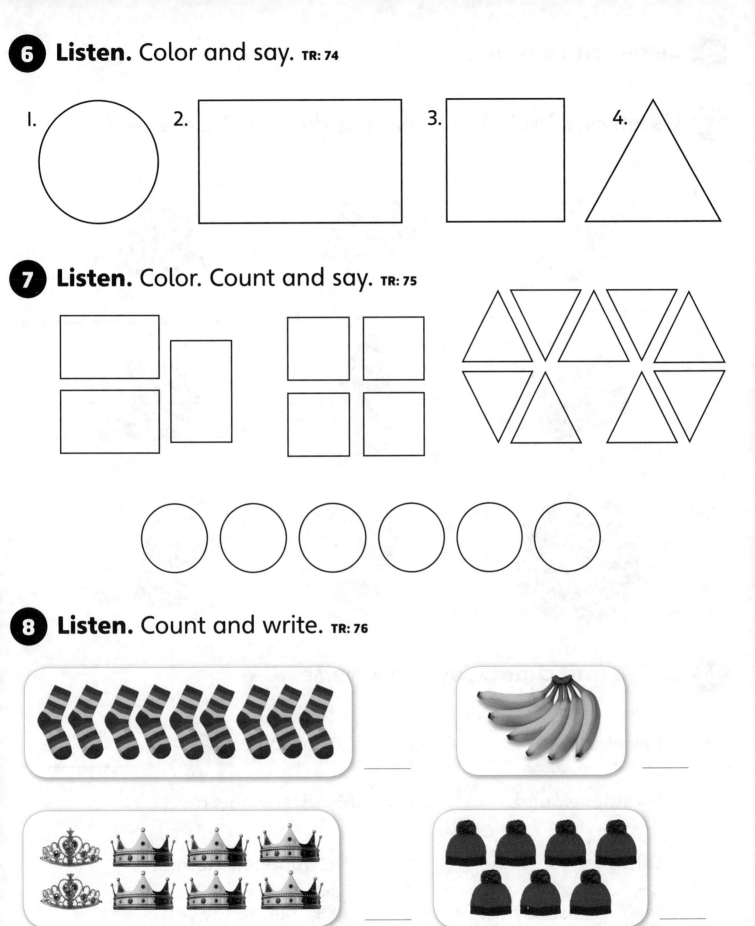

9 **Listen and say.** TR: 77

10 **Listen and look.** Which word is different? Circle. TR: 78

1.

2.

3.

11 **Listen and chant.** Say a new verse. TR: 79

I want a

My sister wants a

Let's shop for clothes.

 please say yes!

I want some

My sister wants a

We want new clothes.

 please say yes!

Unit 8

Animals

1 **Listen and look.** Draw a line. TR: 80

1

2

3

4

5

6

7

8

9

10

2 **Listen and say.** TR: 81

3 **Cut out the cards on page 63.** Listen. Glue the cards. Say. TR: 82

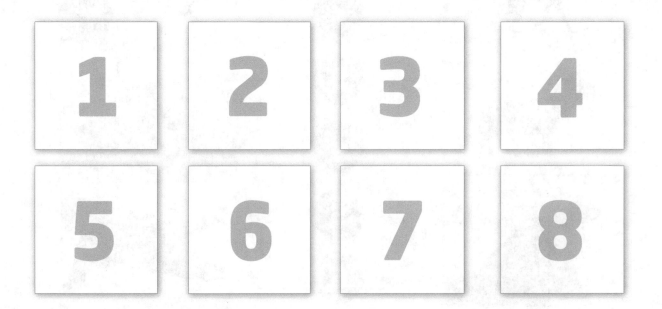

4 **Connect the dots.** What is it? Say. Color.

5 **Listen.** Color and say. TR: 83

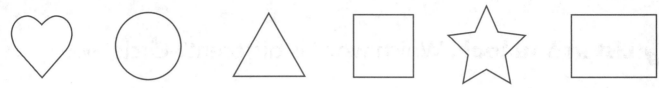

6 **Listen.** Color. Count and say. TR: 84

7 **Listen.** Count and write. TR: 85

8 **Listen and say.** TR: 86

9 **Listen and look.** Which word is different? Circle. TR: 87

1.

2.

3.

10 **Listen and chant.** Say a new verse. TR: 88

Look, I'm a
I walk and I run.

Look, I'm a
standing in the sun.

Look, I'm a
I walk and I run.

Look, I'm a
standing in the sun.

Review

1 **Listen.** Look and circle. TR: 89

1.

2.

3.

4.

5.

6.

7.

8.

2 Listen. Look and circle. TR: 90

1.

2.

3.

3 Listen and color. TR: 91

4 Listen. Count and circle. TR: 92

1.      2.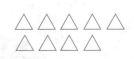

3.   4.

5.   6.

Trace and write.

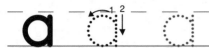

a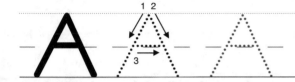

A

b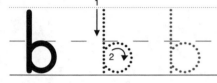

B

apple

paper

book

bye

Trace and write.

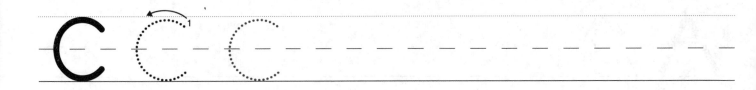

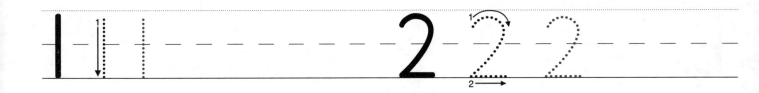

crayon   pencil   chair   car

Trace and write.

d  d d

D 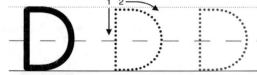 D D

e  e e

E  E E

pen

desk

teddy
bear

Trace and write.

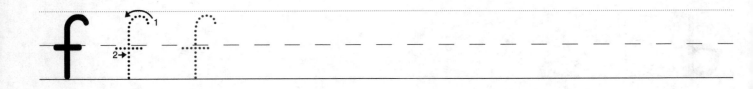

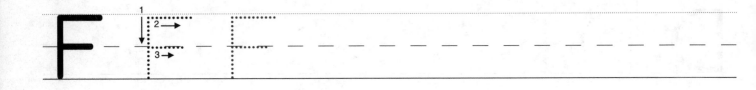

four   eraser   five

Trace and write.

g g g

G G G

h h h

H H H

father

mother

grandma

hello

Trace and write.

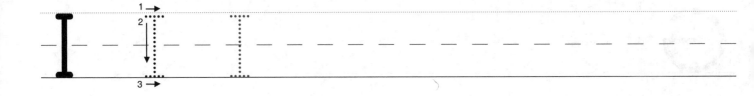

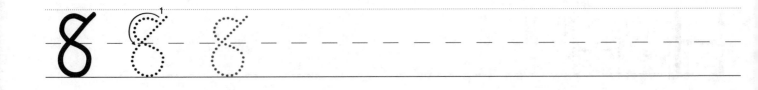

 sisters

 pencil

 Mia

 Eddie

Trace and write.

j   j   j

J   J   J

k   k   k

K   K   K

kite

kitchen

juice

truck

Trace and write.

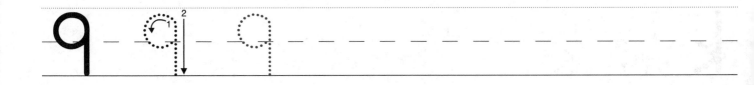

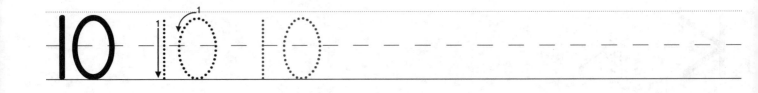

ball   balloon   doll   living room

Trace and write.

m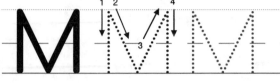

M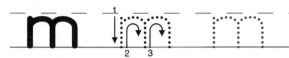

n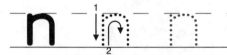

N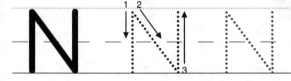

prince   grandma   hands   friends

Trace and write.

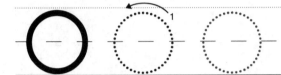

O O O

O O O

nose

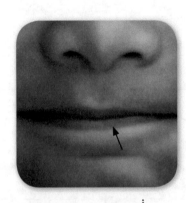

mouth

balloon

bathroom

robot

book

Trace and write.

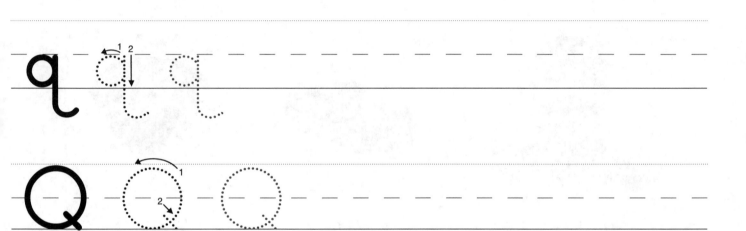

pen   queen   pencil   paper

Trace and write.

r 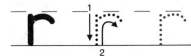 r r

R R R

grandpa

car

rice

prince

bread

cro**w**n

Trace and write.

s s s

S S S

t t t

T T T

 socks

 shorts

 skirt

 shirt

Trace and write.

u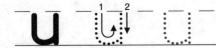

U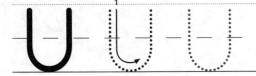

v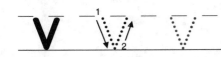

V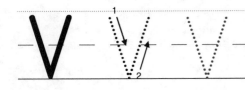

Write your name.

Trace and write.

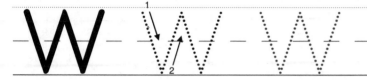

Trace and write.

Use with Unit 8.

y y y

Y Y Y

z z z

Z Z Z

Do you like school?

Yes, I do!

Unit 1   Use with Activity 3 on page 6.

Unit 2   Use with Activity 3 on page 10.

Unit 3 Use with Activity 5 on page 14.

Unit 4 Use with Activity 4 on page 18.

Unit 5   Use with Activity 4 on page 24.

Unit 6   Use with Activity 3 on page 28.

Unit 7 Use with Activity 4 on page 32.

Unit 8 Use with Activity 3 on page 36.